I REMEMBER

MEMORIES FROM LEJAC RESIDENTIAL SCHOOL

MARIAN LYNN DUNCAN

MICHELLE MILLER-GAUTHIER

Tellwell Talent
www.tellwell.ca

ISBN
978-1-83418-167-7 (Hardcover)
978-1-83418-166-0 (Paperback)

Dedication

This book is dedicated to:

- My Granny Mariam Murdock and Grandpa Pete Murdock, who nicknamed me "Ughoo ghoo" which means "born with a tooth" in Dakelh, our traditional language; I was born with two teeth
- All the lost Residential School children and their families
- My children and grandchildren
- Michelle Miller-Gauthier, my friend who helped me with this book

I remember in 1965, on the day I was to leave for Lejac Residential School, Granny Mariam took me shopping for my new clothes. I was almost four years old. We lived in my grandparents' home because my dad went away for work so much, and we moved a lot, so we didn't really have a place to live in Fort St. James.

I remember my granny brought me to the Marshall-Wells store in town. She bought me black velvet shoes and a blue dress.

I remember skipping down the hill and being happy with my new clothes.

I remember one of my favourite things was when Grandpa Pete Murdock sang to me "My Ughoo ghoo" which means "baby teeth." I was born with my two bottom teeth. Even though he had passed away a few months before, the song and his love stayed strong in my mind and heart.

I remember my mom walked into the house. They talked in Dakelh (our language). She took me and led me outside. She put me in a dark car with a driver and got in beside me.

I don't remember the long drive. I didn't know where we were going.

I remember that after a long while, we arrived at a huge building and I was amazed at its size. I wondered what it was and where we were.

My mom opened the back door for me. She told me, "Go knock on the big red door. Let them know you want to visit your brothers and sisters."

I was so excited. All I wanted was to see and be with my brothers and sisters! I hadn't seen them since before the summer when they had been placed in the homes of other family members. Our house had burned down and we had to separate our family.

Little did I know what was about to happen.

I remember that as I knocked on the door, a woman with a long black dress and her head covered opened the door. She asked me, "Where did you come from? How did you get here?"

I remember replying, "With my mom."

I remember I turned to point to where the car was parked.

There was no one around. The car was gone.

I remember that I started to cry.

Later in life I learned that many Indigenous parents had their children taken to Residential Schools by the police. My mom didn't want to have us taken by the police, so she had no choice but to bring me there herself.

I remember I cried as the woman brought me up a stairway, even though I was amazed at the long wooden stairway. Then we came into a huge room full of bunk beds.

She brought me into a huge washroom. I saw rows of sinks. I had never ever seen an indoor toilet before because we only had an outhouse at our home.

She turned on a shower, which I was so afraid of because I had only ever had a bath.

She undressed me and put me in the shower.

She washed me and put some foul-smelling stuff in my hair and dried me off.

I remember she sat me down and cut my hair. I remember crying too hard to be able to see my hair that was falling to the ground. I wanted to go home.

She dressed me in different clothes and took me downstairs to another room, which was full of black and white shoes.

I tried on a few.

When she was satisfied, we made our way down more stairs.

She walked me to a room that was full of other children.

I remember that I was scared and all I could think was *I want to go home.*

I remember my first night there. I still had not seen my brothers and sisters. There were single beds in the middle of the room and bunk beds against the walls. I was put on a top bunk. On the bottom bunk was a girl from Binche, my hometown.

I remember we all cried at night.

The next thing I remember was the lights being turned on and we all had to line up in a single row. Then I heard the first little girl cry out in pain. One by one, we were strapped with a long black thick leather belt because we were all crying for our parents.

Every night this continued until we cried no more.

I remember we had no one to comfort us.

I remember we learned to comfort one another. We would sneak to a crying girl's bed and comfort her quietly because if we got caught, we would be punished.

I remember that when a few older girls tried to talk in their traditional language, they were pulled aside and strapped. The older girls did this on purpose. They wanted to teach us to never say anything in our language, otherwise we would get strapped. Many of us listened to them, but some didn't care and talked back in our language as a way of showing some control over our lives.

My parents never taught me our language. Many children who did know their language lost it because of the rules at Residential School, and we are still working to learn it to this day.

I remember that when we got sick, we had to stay in bed. No one comforted us at all. One of the other girls would bring us meals and leave. When we threw up, we were told to clean it up ourselves with paper towels. Later, someone would bring a small pail for throwing up in.

I remember one of our chores was to clean out the washroom in the junior dorm.

One time, there were three of us cleaning. We had just finished and were very tired. One of the girls went to get the supervisor so she could inspect our work. To our surprise, the supervisor took the mop pail and threw the dirty water all over the washroom. Then, she yelled at us to clean it again!

I remember that our hearts sank and we felt scared and angry with her.

When we were done cleaning the second time, we went to our beds and fell asleep. We had missed supper.

Later that night, we snuck downstairs and took food from the cellar. We took carrots and apples. We snuck this food back upstairs and ate it while everyone else was sleeping

I remember feeling brave for sneaking food.

I remember Lejac Indian Residential School being so different from home. I used to get excited for lineups during mealtimes. Only then would I get to see my older brothers. Boys and girls were separated for all other activities.

I remember great happiness when I saw my siblings. I would sometimes see my older sisters in the hallway and I would wave at them. If no one was looking, we would sneak a hug.

I remember that some days we all had to watch as one of us girls would kneel in the corner with a pencil under her knees for hours.

Another girl would be writing on a full brown paper towel roll "I WILL NOT TALK BACK OR SWEAR" until the whole roll was completed. Some days we'd help the girl and write it down for her, because her fingers would be too sore and cramped up.

I remember that on those days, our spirits were broken to pieces.

I remember that one day at school, I asked to go to the washroom. A nun came out of an upstairs classroom and saw me in the hallway. She grabbed me by the ear and walked fast with me to the office. I leaned on the wall to try to pull away from her as we went. I was the same height as the windowsill, and I hit my head on the window ledge. I got a cut on my eyebrow. She didn't care about it. She just got more upset with me, telling me I deserved it as she took me to the infirmary where I had to get a bandage on my cut.

I remember I cried for my mom and dad. Afterwards, I finally fell asleep on the floor of the classroom. After I woke up, some girls asked what had happened to me. I didn't say anything for fear of getting strapped with the thick black belt.

I remember that fear kept boys and girls broken, tangled spirits silenced for years.

I remember when I was an intermediate student, there were three of us playing outside in the field. I was feeling so suffocated by the punishments given to me and from watching others being punished for such small things, never being able to feel like we could do anything right. I asked them to run away with me. The two girls agreed. We had only the clothes on our backs. We pretended to play army. We slowly made our way down to the railroad tracks. From there, we walked along the tracks until we reached Nadleh Reserve. We met an old man and asked him for directions to the highway. He told us to cross the bridge and keep walking and then we'd see the highway. We continued on. We dared not to walk on the road, so we walked along the bush line. As we walked, it started to grow dark, so we decided to hitchhike. We eventually made it to Fort St. James.

I knew that my granny lived on Wells Street. When we got there, no one was home, so we found what we could eat and fell asleep. I was relieved to be home, but fear was still sneaking up on me because I knew we would get in trouble. Uncle Johnny and Aunty Lillian arrived and were surprised to see us. They asked how we got there, and so we told them we ran away. They told us to go back to sleep.

I remember being very tired but satisfied that we made it home.

The next morning when we got up, we were very scared. Little did we know that my granny had come home late and learned we were there. She got up very early to tell my mom I was at the house with two other girls. The police arrived with my mom. We cursed under our breath as the police started taking us to the car. We were angry and scared to death as we were loaded into the police car and driven back to Lejac.

I remember that having to go back to the school put fear back in my heart.

We knew what was going to happen to us. Other children who had run away were always strapped with a belt when they were brought back to the school.

One by one, we were sent out into the hallway where a male supervisor used his own personal thick black belt. We got twenty lashes each on our behinds.

I remember that I never ran away again.

As the years went by, I grew to know the rest of the girls. Many of us developed a strong bond. The strictness of the school lessened as well, allowing for more lighthearted times. It was around this time that the school started getting rid of the nuns and hiring teachers and staff from local communities, as well as from different countries like England and Ireland. These new people were kinder and gentler than the nuns. They did not punish us the way the nuns had.

In later years, we sometimes camped out on weekends, went swimming in Fraser Lake, and played quite freely on the grounds and in the forest around the school.

Even though holidays were hard if we didn't go home, we got to have some fun celebrations at Christmas and Easter. One time they even hired a magician to entertain us at the Christmas party.

A major highlight for me that helps make some of the difficult memories smaller was being in the Lejac marching band. We travelled to Spokane, Washington, to perform at the 1974 World's Fair. This was the trip of lifetime for me and still burns strong in my mind of happy things from my childhood.

Residential School took away my right to be with my family, and even though things there got a little better, I would rather have been living at home.

I remember missing the delicious food my family would make.

I remember missing home.

I remember missing my grandpa singing to me.

I remember the last time he ever sang his song to me.

Author's Notes

My parents took me and the last three of my siblings out of Lejac Residential School in 1974.

My grandpa passed away in 1965, and I remember being at his wake.

Lejac Friends

Some girls came from my hometown, known as Binche Whut'en. Others were from Portage (Yecooche), Tl'azt'en, Takla, McLeod Lake, Hazelton, Burns Lake (Tsil Kaz Koh), Ingenika (Tsay Keh Dene), and other reserves across Northern British Columbia. Fifty years later, many of us are still in touch. We have supported each other and shared stories with each other as we pieced together our lives and tried to heal from our experiences at Lejac Residential School.

Lejac Residential School was open from 1922 to 1976 on the south shore of Fraser Lake, British Columbia. All children were given a number when they arrived at the school. In an act of reclamation, the site has been renamed Tseyaz Bunk'ut in the local traditional language (Tse -rock; Yaz—little; Bunket—the location off the lake, like an inlet).

About the Author

Marian Duncan is from Binche Whut'en, which is on the shores of Stuart Lake near the geographic centre of what is now known as British Columbia. She is a Residential School Survivor, a mother of five children, and a grandmother to many grandchildren. She has worked in daycares, schools, and a lower mainland twenty-four-hour crisis home supporting Indigenous children. Marian has also worked as a camp cook in the mountains north of Fort St. James, and she has worked in a sawmill. She is a traditional woman who loves hunting, fishing, berry-picking, beading, and other traditional arts. Marian is currently spending her time enjoying her life in Binche, supporting her big family, and writing a book or two.

Manufactured by Amazon.ca
Acheson, AB

17155810R00026